D1451124

THE JOY OF ALLOTMENTS

An illustrated diary of Plot 19

CAROLINE DEPUT

Souvenir Press

First published in Great Britain in 2013 by Souvenir Press Ltd
43 Great Russell Street, London WC1B 3PD

ISBN 9780285642003

Typeset by M Rules

Printed and bound in India by Replika Press Pvt. Ltd.

For Mum

FLOSS' AMAZING

★ALLOTMENT DIARY★

Recording the eternal optimism, often
mis-placed, of keeping a small plot of ★
land sufficiently weeded

watered, manured and hoed in order ★

·····to grow·····

VARIETIES ★ OF ★ VEGETABLES

with alluring names ~ like "Sharpes Express" "Lady
Balfour" ★ "Pink Fir Apple" ★ "Romanesco" ★ "Bull's
Blood."

"Hurst Green Shaft"   "Arctic King"

IT'S EASTER WEEKEND &
FLOSS IS GETTING READY...

AS ALWAYS, AT THE START
OF THE SEASON, SHE HAS
HIGH HOPES OF HER CROPS.

STEVE SUGGESTS A RELAY SYSTEM.
FLOSS IS TO FILL THE BARROW WITH
RUBBISH, HE WILL GO TO THE DUMP.

STEVE HAS TO TAKE THE RUBBISH~
BRANCHES, BROKEN GLASS etc~ TO THE
DUMP, EMPTY THE BAGS, SHOVEL THE
FREE BARK CHIPPINGS FROM THE SKIP,
LOAD THEM INTO THE CAR, THEN PUSH
THEM UP THE LONG PATH.

FLOSS PUT A BAG OF
BARK CHIPPINGS
BACK ON THE BARROW
BY MISTAKE!!!

THIS MEANS STEVE HAS EMPTIED THE
BARK CHIPPINGS FROM THE DUMP BACK
ON TO THE GARDEN WASTE SECTION
AT THE DUMP! OOPSIE!

COLD We still have morning frosts and it's just above freezing. 8°C sometimes during the day~ so quite pleasant in the sunshine if wrapped up. I have decided it is impossible to look stylish on the allotment!

March 7th. Pricked out the Maltese cat-faced tomatoes ~ enough for 15 pots and half a dozen seedlings to spare. Potted on the mini-plug plants bought at Syon Park for the back garden.

Sowed courgettes. Six each of ~
• Black Beauty • Grisette de Provence • Di Nizza • Patty Pan • Golden Zucchini • Yellow Scallop. Sowed in John Innes seed compost, one or two per pot. Placed in heated propagator on back windowsill.

Moved white perennial sweet peas to greenhouse in back garden. Almost all have germinated. Different growth rates though. Some are 2" tall, others only 1/4". I love sweet peas, so I'm hoping the perennial ones are successful.

No chance of getting to the allotment this weekend. The awful cold I had two weeks ago has turned into something worse. Two visits to Dr. da Costa this week.

MARCH

Arch for the runner beans. I saw an article in BBG Gardener's World Magazine which showed runners grown over an arch, over a pathway. A good idea that I might try as it uses a lot less space than wigwams ~ and looks decorative too.

Watercolours. Last week I treated myself to a teeny box of watercolours to use on the allotment. That's if I ever get a moment's peace from the Frenchman Michel. He really doesn't understand that I go to the allotment for SOLITUDE, not for a constant natter!

Maltese tomatoes are now (a week later) in an un-heated propagator in the front bedroom. They germin-ated very quickly, so I moved them when just 1" tall. Better than letting them go "leggy."

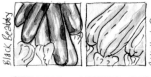

Black Beauty

Grisette de Provence

Di Nizza

Yellow Scallop

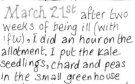

March 21st after two weeks of being ill (with flu), I did an hour on the allotment. I put the kale seedlings, chard and peas in the small greenhouse as it's too damp in the cold frame.

At Kew Gardens some time ago I saw a book on how to paint vegetables in watercolours. I wish I'd bought it as I'm not very good at painting veg ~ a bit of a pain when I'm trying to keep an illustrat-ed diary of my allotment! I did botanical drawing for my O'level art but that was so long ago that I could do with a bit of help.

Looking forward to the growing season getting properly underway. It's a struggle getting things started early enough so they have a long enough growing season, but also trying to stop them from going 'leggy', damping-off or just simply dying!

MARCH 22ND.

Sunshine and a few showers. A balmy 12°c so a lovely day for pottering about

12

Sowed Swiss chard from a VERY OLD packet of seed. And it has germinated! A small triumph of economy for me ~ **HURRAH!**

Applied a general fertilizer of blood, fish and bone to the fruit bushes rather than chicken manure. The foxes adore the chicken manure!

All of the seeds seem to be doing well. The courgettes are either by the window in the front bedroom or in the mini greenhouse on the allotment. The lettuces have come through (sown a few weeks ago) in a half seed tray covered with a cloche and placed in the greenhouse. I carefully checked the max-min thermometer and the coldest it's been is minus 2°c. I am sure I sowed the peas too early and it was too cold for them in the greenhouse. They began to germinate once they were put in the propagator. I planted ten potato tubers - Swift - which are extra earlies. I disturbed a newt when I removed the black plastic that had been over the bed. He seemed to be quite happy and scuttled off; I think he's now in the compost heap.

MIND THE GAP
I've sown kale this year ~ I usually forget! Hopefully I will have some greens later this month to fill the "hungry gap" that happens when waiting for the early Summer.

TOMATOES ???
Good idea? Bad idea? They always seem to end up with blight. Do I sow them? Cheap. Or buy plants? Expensive. I love them, but all that effort for minimum reward? Hmm.

Cos Lettuce

Sow a good selection of salads under cloches now. With enough light as the days start to lengthen, they will germinate quickly. Use as "cut & come again" and leave some to grow on to full size for early salads in the summer.

Compost

START a RUNNER

bean trench. I always forget to do this! With the arch in place over the path, all I have to do is dig a short trench on either side and start to fill it with kitchen waste. The soil is so sandy that the extra bulk should really help.

WHAT TO DO IN
March

TRIM the rosemary that I have trained and clipped into pyramids and spheres. Check the weather forecast for frost first.

PRICK out seedlings as soon as first true leaves develop.

REMOVE seedlings from propagator as soon as they germinate.

SOW squashes in pots only half-filled with compost. Top up as the seedlings reach the top of the pots to encourage better roots and stronger stems.

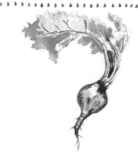

SOW beetroot as soon as the earth is warm.

RED CHICORY
"TREVISO"
Usually sown for an extra early crop under cover. Useful addition to salads but too bitter on it's own, I have found.

Find time to clean hand tools. Oil the handles with a rag that is dipped in oil. Use the same rag to clean the metal parts as well.

Grab

the first fine day to de-clutter the shed. It never takes as long as I think it will and I am always amazed at the amount of space I have in there once it's all tidied up.

Sow

Sea Kale (Lily white) "crambe maritima". I have a packet from "HEIRLOOM AND HERITAGE" seeds which tells me that the Romans ate pickled sea kale to avoid scurvy. I also want to find somewhere that sells samphire seeds. I've read that it is relatively easy to grow. Even if you don't live by the sea, both sea kale and samphire can be grown successfully in pots, so the article claimed.

THERE'S SOMETHING ODD! CAN YOU TRY RADIO 4 FOR THE WEATHER?

AMY FLOSS JOHNSON RADIOS STEVE FOR A WEATHER FORECAST

EXASPERATED, STEVE CHECKS THE WEATHER USING THE TRUSTED CHANNELS

I DON'TKNOW WHY SHE DOESN'T CHECK THE WEATHER BEFORE SHE SETS OFF.

OK. STAY CALM. I'M TUNING IN TO "THE TODAY PROGRAMME" NOW.

THE HOT WEATHER CAUSES SOME CONFUSION ~ it's March and 12°c.

FLOSS IS TOO IMPATIENT. UNABLE TO WAIT FOR STEVE'S REPLY, SHE PANICS AND GOES INTO A SPIN.

"MEEEEEE!"

I CAN'T SEE WHAT THAT ODD THING IS. MY DAY ON THE ALLOTMENT WILL BE RUINED!

FLOSS DECIDES TO BAIL OUT OF HER TRIP TO THE ALLOTMENT

WITHOUT THE WEATHER FORECAST, I NEVER KNOW WHAT TO WEAR FOR THE ALLOTMENT

OH! HELLO! WHAT A NICE SURPRISE. YOU DON'T USUALLY COME TO MEET ME.

HOW AM I GOING TO BREAK IT TO HER THAT THE "ODD THING" WAS THE SUN - AND THAT IT'S GOING TO BE A LOVELY SUNNY DAY?!

STEVE IS UNDERSTANDABLY ANXIOUS. FLOSS STILL HASN'T SEEN THE WEATHER FORECAST.

COLD & WINDY
and wet

Bitterly cold again over the weekend. I have only got in one full day on the allotment. Most of the seeds have started looking rather sorry for themselves. Peas ("Twinkle") sown March 7th came through well in the mini-greenhouse though, and were big enough to be planted out. Put them into a bed which had 2" of compost spread over it first. The 24 courgette seedlings are down to about a dozen in the allotment mini greenhouse ~ a combination of cold and slugs. Maltese cat ~

APRIL

the cruelest month

COLD WET WINDY

faced tomatoes, again in the mini greenhouse, seem to be doing well. I took a cloth and window cleaner up there and thoroughly cleaned the greenhouse and cold frame. Having spent a good half an hour pricking out 48 tiny lettuce,

I was livid when I dropped them ~ and knocked over the beetroot and celeriac seedlings ~ all over the floor of the newly-cleaned greenhouse!

Plantings ~

  Potatoes ~ Salads, First Earlies and mains.

  Under netting ~

    Broad beans saved from seed last year, sown in newspaper tubes and transplanted to top of the plot.

    Kale (Hungry Gap) grown on for two weeks in the greenhouse

Note. Winter Kale seems to do better under cover on the allotment.

Grown on for two weeks, these became big healthy plants, 5" tall.

The seedlings at home remained just that ~ seedlings!

Second week April

At last. 17°c. Sunshine. Clear skies. 1st radishes (sown 28th Feb). Sowings now should only take 3 weeks before ready. Little Gem lettuces in cloche are now starting to form hearts. A few carrots (also sown 28th Feb under the cloche) are starting to come up.

Squashes (were a dozen) now down to 6 in the greenhouse ~ slugs! Sowed winter squashes; a full tray of beetroot; a dozen sunflowers ("Black Magic") in the main greenhouse.

State of crops...

~ KALE (Hungry Gap) 8"-12" tall under nets.
~ PEAS (Twinkle) 6" tall
~ BROAD BEANS all sown direct, are growing well
~ ASPARAGUS no sign yet
~ GARLIC is looking drawn & yellow
~ WINTER LETTUCE in cloche are now forming nice hearts
~ SWISS CHARD under glass looks fit & healthy
~ SPINACH is springing into life

State of crops

~ SEAKALE finally germinated.
~ RED CAULIFLOWERS, sown early March, have caught up with DECEMBER sowings

TASKS

~ Completely emptied one of the top compost bins. I carefully sieved it onto the dahlia bed & added the stones & debris to the paths.
~ Tidied all the brambles from the blackberries for burning.
~ Planted the last of the potatoes. Weeded all the paths.

OBSERVATIONS

~ GREENGAGE is smothered in blossom ~ the most I've ever seen.
~ PLUM just breaking into blossom.
~ GOOSEBERRIES - buds breaking.
~ WOODPECKERS - lots this year, both the green & the red ones
~ FRENCHMAN continues to stockpile Argos catalogues to fill the waist-deep trench he has dug.

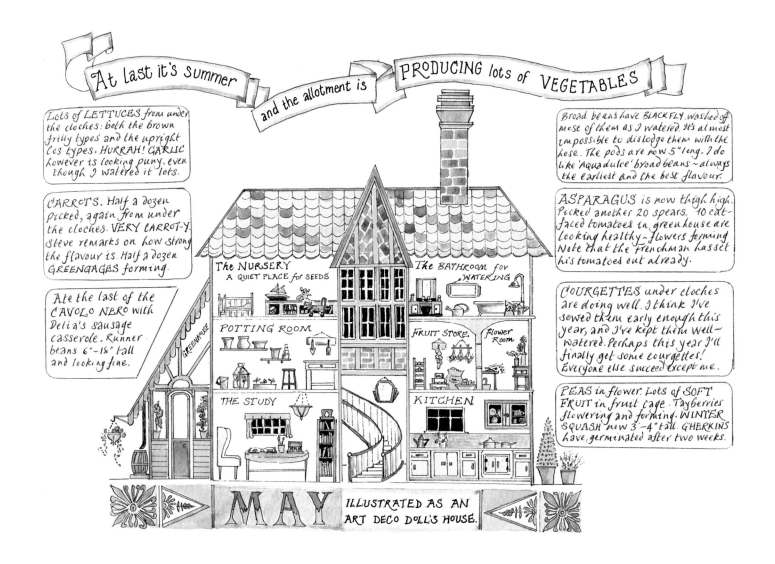

At last it's summer and the allotment is PRODUCING lots of VEGETABLES

Lots of LETTUCES from under the cloches: both the brown frilly types and the upright Cos types. HURRAH! GARLIC however is looking puny, even though I watered it lots.

CARROTS. Half a dozen picked, again from under the cloches. VERY CARROT-Y. Steve remarks on how strong the flavour is. Half a dozen GREENGAGES forming.

Ate the last of the CAVOLO NERO with Delia's sausage casserole. Runner beans 6"-18" tall and looking fine.

Broad beans have BLACKFLY. Washed off most of them as I watered. It's almost impossible to dislodge them with the hose. The pods are now 5" long. I do like 'Aquadulce' broad beans ~ always the earliest and the best flavour.

ASPARAGUS is now thigh high. Picked another 20 spears. 10 cat-faced tomatoes in greenhouse are looking healthy ~ flowers forming. Note that the Frenchman has set his tomatoes out already.

COURGETTES under cloches are doing well. I think I've sowed them early enough this year, and I've kept them well-watered. Perhaps this year I'll finally get some courgettes! Everyone else succeed except me.

PEAS in flower. Lots of SOFT FRUIT in fruit cage. Tayberries flowering and forming. WINTER SQUASH now 3"-4" tall. GHERKINS have germinated after two weeks.

GREENHOUSE

The NURSERY
A QUIET PLACE for SEEDS

The BATHROOM for WATERING

POTTING ROOM

FRUIT STORE.

Flower Room

THE STUDY

KITCHEN

MAY
ILLUSTRATED AS AN ART DECO DOLL'S HOUSE.

Mr. Badger

No tayberries. Mr Badger has forced his way into the fruit cage, trashed the canes, eaten the tayberries and trampled on the few berries he didn't devour.

Floss is not happy. It's the beginning of June and the month is off to a bad start.

June

No rain for weeks! Only one day when there was any rain to speak of but the downpour made no difference.

We went on holiday for a week to the lovely Xara Palace. June is never a good time to leave the allotment to its own devices.

The plot is tinder dry! The rose is rampant ~ as is the bindweed ~ and the blackberry is like the forest that sprung up round Sleeping Beauty!

The birds got at the gooseberries before I had the chance to pick them! I MUST remember to net them next year. The birds also got into the fruit cage. I don't think I'm doing very well this year.

Blackfly is the worst I've ever seen. Despite constantly washing it off the broad beans and pinching out the tops, they are all shrivelled.

Something has dug up the Jerusalem artichokes ~ how odd! The sweet peas are burnt to a crisp and the sunflowers are twigs.

OH NO! One week away and nature's taken over.

"YUM"

It turns out that the double row of dwarf French beans that I sowed are not dwarf French beans ~ they are CLIMBING French beans! This means I have to carefully put in canes, then untangle the beans and tie them up the canes. Idiot!

SUCCESS! Cauliflowers look great.

Planted out the tomatoes & took the cloches off the courgettes. Weeded the asparagus bed

1st week of July

At last, a full day on the allotment. Everything is parched~the lawn, the ground, the paths~everything. I picked 5 lbs of redcurrants though. When the sun has shone on them and they are warm, the taste is up there with tomatoes. I sowed radishes and purple sprouting broccoli.

There are no potatoes this year~a combination of late frosts and summer heat. A real shame, but it's just one of those things. Steve helped me pull up the bindweed~ I just caught him in time as he moved towards the tendrils wound around some poles~the runner beans.

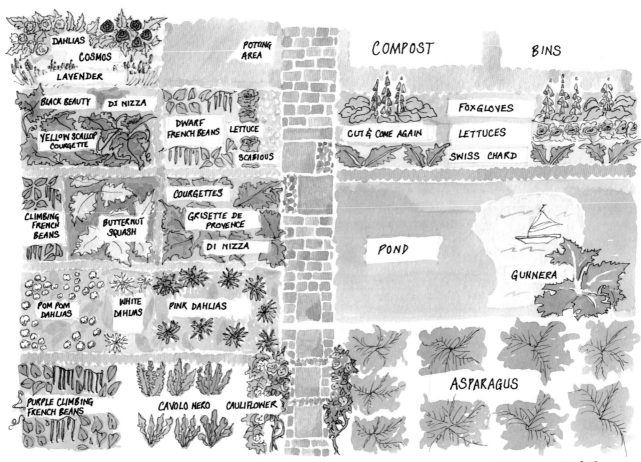

SPRING ONIONS

LETTUCE

BRASSICAS

VACANT (left under black plastic all season)

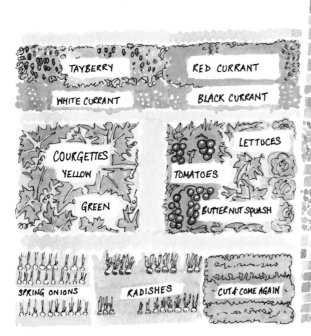
TAYBERRY

RED CURRANT

WHITE CURRANT

BLACK CURRANT

COURGETTES
YELLOW

GREEN

LETTUCES

TOMATOES

BUTTER NUT SQUASH

SPRING ONIONS

RADISHES

CUT & COME AGAIN

TOP PLOT JULY

WHITE
GLADIOLI

BLACK CURRANT

TOMATOES

LETTUCES

GREEN MANURE

GOOSE BERRIES

BEETROOT   CELERIAC   RADISHES   CAVOLO NERO

MIXED LETTUCES

GREEN-
GAGE

BEET ROOTS

SALADS

PLUM

PEARS

APPLES

JULY

~ VEGETABLES IN BUCKETS ~

CABBAGES Sow half a packet into a bucket in late July or early August. Add a sprinkling of lime to the compost before sowing. Start the seeds off outside, and they will germinate in around 7 days. Once they are 6" high, thin & use as baby veg. Right, I've tried this before and the slugs got to them, so this year I'm using slug bait as soon as they go into the greenhouse at the beginning of September.

KALE Last winter, I left some Cavolo Nero seedlings in the mini greenhouse by mistake and over the cold months, they turned into beautiful big healthy plants. It turns out that quite a few others on the allotments do this so I've looked it up in one of my gardening magazines. You start off your Kale in late summer, then transplant them to 3-4 per big pot or bucket. Water sparingly. The advantages are two~fold. The pigeons are kept at bay (as long as you close the greenhouse door!) And the plants seem to grow a lot bigger, faster.

ONIONS Autumn sets are the best for this. Starting in the middle of a big pot (bucket-sized) filled with compost, place the onion sets in nice, neat concentric circles. They should just touch. After 3 weeks they should have put on growth so water them. Put in the greenhouse and use like salad onions.

SALADS. I love Lamb's lettuce, so I might try sowing some this week. I've succeeded in the past by using a small plastic ice cream tub with holes punched in the bottom. I think lots of light is beneficial too.

CARROTS I never have much success with carrots. Eve on the neighbouring plot just seems to sow ~ and they grow. Sown in buckets in July/August, you should get baby ones for Christmas.

POTATOES are not as easy as everyone makes them out to be! I think you really do need a proper, draught-proof greenhouse to get a decent crop. Mine just spend the winter in a deep sulk!

FLOSS HAS DECIDED...

...AFTER MEASURING UP...

...THAT SHE WILL WALLPAPER...

...THE SPARE WALL OF THE
GREENHOUSE!

I don't think it's too "loud."

WEATHER still no rain. A couple of heavy cloud bursts ~ and that's been it. I've watered thoroughly every time I've visited the allotment, sometimes spending over an hour directing the hose onto the plants' roots.

· · · · · · · · · · · · · · ·

SOWED two rows of beetroot, Swiss chard, Cavolo Nero and radishes on the top plot. I mixed in the last of the Grow More first. I often don't have much success sowing seed direct. The germination rate is often poor. I buy seeds in the belief that it must be cheaper than buying plug plants, but I've started to wonder if this is a false economy. So this time I've sowed the seeds more thickly, at the rate of two short rows per packet.

· · · · · · · · · · · · · · ·

TRANSPLANTED lettuces (mixed "FRANCHINI" seeds) from the bottom plot, puddling them in, in front of the yellow beans and the French beans in a spare patch.
I've also had a go a transplanting radishes. I watered them in well in the hope that they would take.
(Turns out they do ~ ready in August).

JULY
WARTIME GUIDE
1/6

Issued in support of
FLOSS' WAR ON WEEDS and her "KEEP THE BADGERS OFF THE TAYBERRIES" CAMPAIGN.

by Floss Deput
Edited by Rubydoo

July special edition

PICKED the first blackberries of the season. Pruning out the old wood every autumn is a real pain (literally!) but it pays off. I notice the neighbours' children help themselves. I suppose they think that because the blackberries are close to the main path, they must be fair game. I wonder if I should say something but decide to hold my tongue ~ I don't want them to think I'm a mean old witch!

· · · · · · · · · · · · · · ·

HARVESTED three purple cauliflowers. Delicious flavour but they haven't been as successful as in previous years, probably because we haven't had enough rain. Also picked

- 30 black climbing French beans
- 3 courgettes
- 1 tomato (ordinary)
- 3 cat-faced tomatoes
- First runner beans of the season
- More Swiss chard
- First dahlias (pink & "Arabian Night"

· · · · · · · · · · · · · · ·

FRUSTRATIONS The Frenchman has excavated a huge mound of earth which has collapsed onto my plot. I'll have to have a word with him...

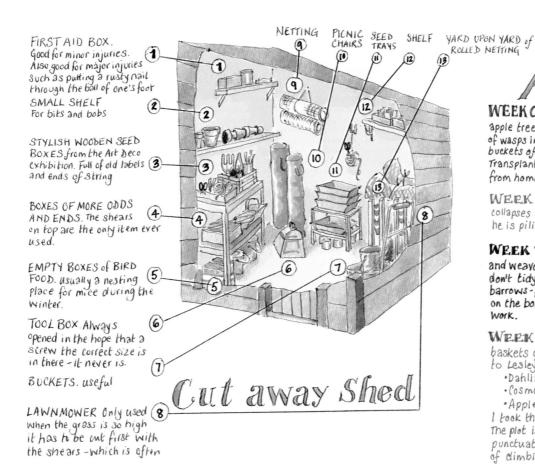

FIRST AID BOX. Good for minor injuries. Also good for major injuries such as putting a rusty nail through the ball of one's foot — ①

SMALL SHELF For bits and bobs — ②

STYLISH WOODEN SEED BOXES from the Art Deco exhibition. Full of old labels and ends of string — ③

BOXES OF MORE ODDS AND ENDS. The shears on top are the only item ever used. — ④

EMPTY BOXES of BIRD FOOD. Usually a nesting place for mice during the winter. — ⑤

TOOL BOX. Always opened in the hope that a screw the correct size is in there – it never is. — ⑥

BUCKETS. useful — ⑦

LAWNMOWER Only used ⑧ when the grass is so high it has to be cut first with the shears – which is often

NETTING ⑨
PICNIC CHAIRS ⑩
SEED TRAYS ⑪
SHELF ⑫
YARD UPON YARD of ROLLED NETTING ⑬

Cut away Shed

AUGUST

WEEK ONE Removed bindweed from apple trees. Watered for 2 hours. No sign of wasps in compost bin, so added 2 buckets of comfrey and watered it well. Transplanted 4 rows of mixed lettuce from home.

WEEK TWO The Frenchman's fence collapses under the weight of earth he is piling against it.

WEEK THREE. I build cloches and weave a small fence, but I still don't tidy the shed! I did sift two barrows-ful of compost from the bin on the bottom plot ~ back breaking work.

WEEK FOUR Picked two baskets of produce and gave one to Lesley and Philip
- Dahlias
- Cosmos
- Apples
- Runner beans
- French beans
- Garlic

I took the netting off the squashes. The plot is a sea of squashes, punctuated with soaring pyramids of climbing beans.

SEPTEMBER

2nd week

Picked two bags of French beans which had appeared from nowhere while we were in Yorks. for a week. There was no sign of them before we left – now there are armful!

Harvested more lettuces. Cos types a great success this year – sowing thickly really helps. 2 doz big fat round radishes. We eat this for lunch over the next week – I forgot about mine and Steve found them sprouting in my lunch box a week or so later!

Weeded under all the cloches.

Cut 2 huge bunches of dahlias. The dark pompom ones are just coming into their own. Like the man at Chelsea Flower Show said when I bought my lilies – everything is a month late this year after the harsh winter we had.

State of crops:
Cavolo Nero benefited from being sown thickly ie entire packet in a short row & being covered by a netting cloche. Now needs thinning out.
Purple sprouting broccoli set out under netting cloche on top plot
Yellow beans JUST starting to flower – I obviously sowed them too late!
Potatoes in greenhouse are now waist high!

Swiss chard which I transplanted (6-7 per pot, 2 pots) are putting on growth in the greenhouse.

Sowed onion sets, 100 per pot, 2 pots. Red & brown sets bought from Wilkies. Brown ones from Reighton Nurseries – "Radar" & suitable for forcing. Also sowed SPRING cabbage in pot. Suggested sowing rate 60 per pot. Packet said 40. Only 20 inside!

Added chicken pellets to onions but forgot lime when sowing the spring cabbage!

CTOBER, second week. Harvested the squash, the ones that had been under the net cloches until the third week of August. They are a round squash, not butternut squash at all! It turns out this diary is useless! The entry for the second week in April merely informs me that I have sown "6 winter squash." Would have helped if I'd said what sort! Anyway, whatever type they are, I have 12 of them. I store 6 of them in the greenhouse, bring 3 home and give 1 to Lesley and Philip.

I prune the blackberry which takes 3 hours. This involves tying all the prunings into neat bundles for burning. It's cold but sunny so I continue to cut everything back. I trim the rosemary, thyme and sage. I also prune the climbing roses and the honeysuckle. No one has seen the Frenchman for ages. I still don't know what to do about the fence. He said he'd fix it, and he has all the materials but he has disappeared.

Oooh, the drama! Kathy's plot is over-run with school kids, swinging on the fruit cage and chucking pots and canes all over the place. I march across and ask them what on earth they are doing. (Actually what I say is "Oi! You lot. Hop it!") "It's our plot," they retort. After trying to persuade them otherwise, I ask to see their supervisor. (Do I think I'm in Waitrose?! I meant to say "teacher" but I'm a bit wound up by this point.)

Their teacher appears. "Must've got the wrong plot," he mumbles. He makes no apology and shuffles off, followed by his rowdy charges who seem more interested in destruction than horticulture.

I fed the lawn a couple of weeks ago and with all the rain and sunny intervals, it's now almost knee-high! The lettuces have been a success this year – the Lollo Rosso types have been particularly tasty and even the Cos types have heartened up. I think we've only had to buy a couple of lettuces all summer.

Another success has been the French beans – both the dwarf types and the climbing ones. We have had them in salads – fresh and frozen. The black climbing ones haven't been so good though. They matured too quickly between pickings.

Using the mesh cloches has also helped my brassicas. They keep the pigeons off the seedlings and seem to deter the foxes from digging latrines. Not entirely, but enough to make life bearable.

I spent much of today cutting back the climbers and shrubs but I also repaired the mini-greenhouse and nailed some thin strips of wood to the main greenhouse to exclude the draughts. I'm hoping that the oilskin table covers that I used to "wallpaper" the back walls of the greenhouse will also help to keep the draughts out. It looks a bit bonkers but I've grown to like it!

Weather. A mere 4°c, but sunny. The first day on the allotment in my week off work. The weather has been dire! Very cold and continuous rain. Wednesday (today) is the first time it's been warm and dry enough to go to the plot.

Transplanted twenty spring cabbages onto the bed by the rhubard (eh? Is that a cross with Swiss chard! I meant "rhubarb!") Bought at Reighton Nurseries as seedlings, there were 12 per pot. I think I paid 69p per pot, so they were rather good value ~ that's if they grow, of course! I put down some Growmore first, and remembered to put down the lime as well. Covered two rows with mesh cloche and put chicken wire cloches over the remainder.

1ˢᵗ week November ~ *Autumn Winds.*

Cut down all the dahlias; it's always a shame. Covered them with the asparagus fern. Sounds like a five minute job when you put it like that! More like two hours of chopping, composting and weeding first the two dahlia beds and then the huge asparagus bed (24 crowns of asparagus and about the same number of dahlias). A dozen new potatoes from the greenhouse **Hurrah!** at last. Are tiny but look delicious. Also a big armful of Swiss chard.

Harvested 12 Milan purple top turnips (had lost the label and thought they were rocket!) A dozen new potatoes from

Observations. Transplanting brassicas to the two greenhouses seems to work, as they are now nearly ready the same row as those now in the greenhouses. The ones outside are a third of the size, and come from the same row as those now in the greenhouses.

DADAH!

A PLAN An Account Planner's (that's my day job) plan for a three year rotation

plan for my plot in Richmond. At last! I'm organised!

TOP PLOT

BOTTOM PLOT

FIR TREE

COMPOST

BLACKCURRANT

GLADIOLI

GREENHOUSE AND COLD FRAME

COMPOST BINS

1 BRASSICAS POTATOES SALADS

6 TOMATOES SQUASH SALADS

10 SQUASH POTATOES

11 SALADS BROAD BEANS

16 SALADS BROAD BEANS ONIONS

2 BROAD BEANS BRASSICAS POTATOES

7 CLIMBING BEANS BRASSICAS POTATOES

BEANS

BRASSICAS

FRUIT CAGE

GOOSEGOGS

12 SQUASH TOMS

13 SQUASH ROOTS

POND

COURGETTE TOMS BROAD BEANS BRASSICAS

8 BRASSICAS TOMATOES RUNNER BEANS

GREENGAGE

BEANS then SALAD

TOMS

ASPARAGUS
good as 'soldiers'

3   **4**

9 BRASSICAS FRENCH BEANS SQUASH

PLUM

DAHLIAS

5 ONION & then RADISH   TOMATOES   BRASSICAS

BRASSICAS SALADS ROOTS **14**

BRASSICAS then BEANS SALADS ROOTS **15**

FOXGLOVES

APPLES
under-planted with daffodils.

PALM

RHUBARB

■ 2010   ▨ 2011   ▰ 2012

Observations.

A better crop rotation plan might be needed for next year.

The brassicas are in a right old muddle again! THE CAVOLO NERO, ALTHOUGH A GREAT SUCCESS, IS RARELY PLANNED FOR, BEING SOWN LATER IN THE SEASON IN JUNE. CURLY KALE SEEMS TO BE ANOTHER SUCCESS THIS YEAR. I'VE NEVER MANAGED WITH IT BEFORE NOW.

Creating a plan twice a year is a better idea I suspect. REMEMBERING TO DO IT WILL BE DIFFICULT.

I THINK a good plan might be to make a three year rotation plan, putting everything in blocks ie. all the brassicas together, all the root crops together etc, and have it all worked out in advance. I could add a six monthly element to it as well.

Six month cycle would allow me to factor in those pesky late-season brassicas! Hey, what's not to like about this cunning new planning-plan, eh?

I SUSPECT I SHOULD GO BACK TO SOME OF MY MANY GARDENING BOOKS, RATHER THAN TRY TO WORK IT OUT MYSELF. OTHERWISE I COULD END UP IN A RIGHT OLD MUDDLE, FORGETTING THAT RADISHES ARE MEMBERS OF THE BRASSICA FAMILY, AND THINKING LETTUCES ARE RELATED TO CARROTS (ARE THEY?)

LIKE all the other plans I make, this plan for a plan will probably never see the light of day! Hey, how well I know myself!

SNAKES and LADDERS 2010
END
WHAT DID I DO??
"Now look here, mate..."
BADGERS ate pretty much all of the soft fruit this year.
WORKED TOO MANY FRIDAYS.
impatient drumming of fingers.
SQUASH A BIG SUCCESS~ the Winter ones in particular.
SWEET PEAS. Not a single one! No marrowfat peas either.
Adding compost meant less watering.
BEANS WERE LIKE SOMETHING from "JACK & THE BEANSTALK" (French, runner & broad).
Managed to grow lettuces by the bucketful. Hurrah!
"I do wish she'd concentrate!"
WEATHER Everything off to a late start. Then NO RAIN for weeks in the summer.
Sub-zero in Jan.
START.

NOVEMBER

Annual Report

Broad beans do better when sown in November ~ direct or as transplants. They beat the droughts and blackfly when sown in Autumn.

Lambs' lettuce works when sown in cold frame in November. It doesn't work as a Winter cut-and-come-again, but does work as an early Spring, gloriously fresh and green first salad of the year (small crop, lasting only two weeks though).

Arctic King, again, fabulous for overwintering, for cropping in March/April.

Potatoes ~ beware the frosts! Buy from the Organic Gardening Catalogue ~ they are ALWAYS better, and don't plant too early.

Straw-y horse manure must be kept wet to stop wasps / hornets moving in.

Sow squashes early. Sowing in March gave them plenty of time to get big enough before planting out. Half-filling the pots with compost, then "earthing up" also worked.

So, that's a whole twelve months of the allotment diary.
Like Harry in the BBC's 'Victorian Kitchen Garden' it's time to wave goodbye to the last year.

end of year

Guest appearance
Steve

Also staring
The Badgers..as themselves
The Slugs....as themselves
The Aphids.as themselves
FLOSS....Caroline J.Deput

FILMED ON LOCATION
IN GLORIOUS

A PICTURE BOOK
····◆◆◆····
FOR MODERN TIMES

Now a major
film

" The sprouts blew
me away "
★ ★ ★ ★
PLOT HOLDERS' MONTHLY

"She knows her
onions "
★ ★ ★ ★
ALLOTMENT LIVING

"Not nec-e-celery
everyone's
cup of tea "
★
CELERY GROWERS' INC.

" Curiously constrained
cultivation of carrots"
★ ★
ALLITERATION ALMANAC

12 CONTAINS STRONG
VEGETABLES

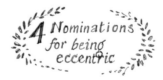

ON YOUR MARKS, 2011 GET SET, GO!

Oh yes, it's the start of the new gardening year.

REMEMBER, "THE DAYS PASS SLOWLY BUT THE YEARS RUN QUICKLY," DIFFICULT TO ACKNOWLEDGE AT THIS TIME OF YEAR WHEN I AM ITCHING TO GET ON THE ALLOTMENT & START GROWING.

ASPARAGUS

WILL NEED REPLACINIG SOON

I think that the **GROMLIN** variety I currently have is called but it's no longer available.

We've had the asparagus bed since we first got the allotment and it's now starting to get a bit "tiered." We can only harvest it for 6 short weeks each year; I can't believe the last 11 years have gone so fast.

I'M FULL OF O P T I M I S M BUT I ALWAYS AM AT THE START OF EVERY YEAR. THE BARE EARTH IS A BLANK CANVAS WAITING FOR

Peas + Beans + Pak Choi + Lettuce + Spuds + everything!

January 2011

I'm trying to work out if January is my least favourite month. It's so cold and wet that there is no point in even trying to do anything on the allotment. I haven't been up there since November when I cut back the dahlias. I suspect that the 3 rows of broad beans that I sowed will have either been eaten by the mice, or will have shrivelled in all the snow that we've had. I sowed a dozen broad beans in the cold frame in the back yard on the 1st of January, so I'm hoping they might survive and replace the ones on the allotment. That's if the mice don't eat those, too!

Yes, on balance, I think that January must be my least favourite month. Every gardening book that I pick up has very few pages devoted to this month, while the gardening magazines suggest reading a gardening book in January! Have the journalists and editors of these magazines never picked up a gardening book and turned to the few, and sparsely populated, pages which relate to January!

I did get some lovely garden-related Christmas presents, though.

A couple of pairs of RHS gold gloves ~ one waterproof and the other very warm. Plus a set of secateurs from Jennie, to replace the ones I left on the front path, begging to be stolen ~ and of course, they were!

WEEDED the top allotment WHICH TOOK AGES.

PRUNED THE GOOSEBERRIES TAKING OUT ALL THE DEAD WOOD

FOUND the mice have not only moved in on the bird seed, they've actually moved in to it. I'm daft. I'd left the lid off the tin. WHAT AN IDIOT I AM!

Trimmed the bay

Dug a runner bean trench and added a bucketful of vegetable peelings from home ~ a paltry amount that barely covered the bottom. I added the last of the manure, too.

THERE WERE FIVE BUCKETS OF MANURE, ENOUGH TO FILL THE RUNNER TRENCH

Do I get free manure from the stables again? Bulky to transport & takes a year to rot. Or, do I pay £15 for four bags from Homebase? We have a bigger boot on the new car, so I could experiment with both bought and free manure and see which performs the best.

FIXED THE NETTING ON THE FRUIT CAGE. IT WAS CAUGHT ON THE WEATHER VANE AND I HAD TO STRETCH WITH A CANE TO REACH IT. THE CAGE IS NOW Badger-Proof at the base. Picked the first daffodils.

FEBRUARY 4th

Courgette

Sowed a mixture of black, green and round courgettes, 2 seeds per pot. Also patty pans and yellow ones.

SOW under cover RADISH
SHORT ROWS

RADISH. 4 short rows under the big cloche.
PEAS "TWINKLE." Again, 4 short rows under the big tunnel cloche but with Growmore added
BROAD BEANS. 24 pots of 'Aqua Dulce', 2 seeds per pot and then into the cold frame. Hoping the mice don't get them...

WEATHER
HARD TO PREDICT, PERENNIAL

COLD. Only 5-6°c. Either damp and grey, or buckets of cold rain. One day of glorious hazy sunshine mid-week (no use to a gardener who is in an office during the week). Itching to get onto the allotment.

GUARANTEE Changeable weather to be expected in Feb.

FEBRUARY 11th
TIME TO SOW.

VERSAILLES TETRA
[COSMOS]

Sowed Versailles Tetra & mixed colours of Cosmos. Two per module, 24 modules in total. Am growing them among the dahlias as cutting flowers for home.

Best Before Aug 2014

£2.40

TOMATO

Sown in warm moist compost, two per 3" pot. These will go in the greenhouse so I am hoping that I haven't sown them too early in the year.

GARDENER'S DELIGHT

TURN FEB-MAR

Compost

WHILE sorting through my bank statements, I found the details which Kathy had given me for the Compost Centre, out near Woking. She's ordered from there before. Not only do they deliver to allotments (many don't), but the delivery is free!

An 80 litre bag is £2.45, which makes it far more economical than the garden centre. Once we have ordered new wood for the raised beds, we'll order some compost from them. 20 bags?

SPECIAL OFFER

March

second week. The palm tree on the allotment has shed so many leaves. They won't compost, so I've been tying them into bundles to go to the tip. Then I had an idea ~ weave them into a fence! It takes an hour to do just one panel 2½'high and about as wide. At this rate, it'll take me about three years just to do the top half of the allotment...

Under, over...
...under, over

Another mile or so to go!

While I'm in re-cycling mode, I find a use for the rope from Millie's & Ruby's old scratching post. There's yards of it, and as it's quite rough & hairy, I reckon it would make a good support for runner beans. I knot it into squares, like the net on a kid's rope climbing frame and attach it to the runner bean arch I made last year. I also find time to tidy the shed. This year the mice have nested in a fleece tunnel cloche. It is, of course, ruined as the mice have shredded it to a pulp for their cosy nest.

March

Sowed "Marmande" tomatoes.
They should be like the cat-faced tomatoes we have in Malta. Confident in my new-found propagator skills, I sow them in modules, and pop them into the heated propagator. As soon as they germinate, I whip them out. But it's another "Ooops!" I've not labelled them correctly~they are Brussel Sprouts!

Labels
I'm starting to wonder what else I've put the wrong labels on... as well as whether ANY of the tomatoes that have germinated are "Marmande."

Weather
No rain! Every thing is tinder dry. I will have to buy some compost or manure before long, otherwise nothing will grow.

Am learning
from my mistakes. You would have thought that 10 years was long enough to have got the hang of the propagator... but I've never mastered it until now. Speaking to Mum, I need to take out things the moment they show through. Now I'm like a cook who's just discovered how the fan oven works.

Lettuces
oops! I sowed a quarter tray in the propagator and promptly forgot about them. A week later, they were through but baked into little threads of "shrivelled~ness."

I start again...

Pak choi is PROMISING
It germinated quickly and is looking strong.

MARCH

Busy, busy, busy. The plastic greenhouse in the back yard is FULL! I've got cabbages, lettuces, broad beans, peas, pak choi, tomatoes, cosmos, snapdragons, bedding dahlias and sweet peas.

I've planted a bed of potatoes called "International Kidney." They're Jersey Royals but can only be called that if grown in Jersey. Because I lost all my potatoes to the frost last year, I'm taking no chances and have covered them in black plastic to keep them snug. I put down organic slug pellets under the plastic first ~ they do like to hide and breed anywhere damp, warm and dark. Two weeks later, the first potato shoots are coming through and I can remove the plastic.

No sign of the Frenchman. I haven't seen Robin for ages, either (the plot is actually Robin's). I've planted out the sweet peas-hope it's not too early.

The peas, lettuce and radishes under the cloche are looking very healthy. I've thinned out the radish and lettuce every week; it's fiddly but they grow so much better when I remember to do this. The greenhouse isn't nearly as draughty now that it's wall-papered. We used to have a big walk-in plastic and metal greenhouse. It was brilliant until one winter when the wind got under it and it took off like a zeppelin ~ landing four plots away!

20 x 80 litre bags of good compost were delivered to the cemetery gates today. Cathy left a message to tell me (we'd split an order with the aptly named "Compost Centre" a week or so ago). The Council are pretty strict about us allotment holders using the cemetery gate for access ~ rightly so. If I left a big stack of bagged compost there for long, I'd be ticked-off. I was working from home when I got Cathy's message, so I raced round to Lesley's to get my bicycle, and with a kitchen apron over my work clothes, I cycled up to the allotment at top speed. It was 27°c. Baking! It took me a whole hour to trundle back and forth with the 20 bags ~ in such heat!

Brock and Alice were both sitting on Brock's plot next to the cemetery gate, sipping cold wine in the late afternoon sun. It made my journeys

feel even longer! Hey ho... We picked the first of the asparagus the 2nd week in April. By the 4th week we are cutting it midweek to keep up ~ leave it 5 days and there are 60 to pick.

4th week in April and I pick the last of the Cavolo Nero, and armsful (?) of perpetual spinach and Swiss Chard. 3rd week in April and I removed the asparagus fern that I had put over the dahlias for the winter. I break it up, as it's dry, and put it on the paths. Glad that I thought of a use for it, as it takes forever to rot down in the compost bins. The first buds are starting to show on the climbing rose. Plant out broad beans sown at home and sow a very old packet of salsify - three weeks later and there's no signs of life.

Illustration text: SOW SALADS UNDER COVER · SOW SPINACH · ASPARAGUS · PICK CAVOLO NERO · CHARD · BAGS OF COMPOST TO BE TAKEN ON THE HOTTEST DAY OF APRIL · SOW JERSEY ROYALS · SOW SWEET PEAS · ROYAL BLUE · SOW SALSIFY IN DRILLS · MULCH BROAD BEANS · WARM SOIL

APRIL

Recorded as a LETTUCE

May

There's been no rain to speak of since early March! We're all waiting for a hosepipe ban. For once I'm following the advice from the gardening gurus i.e. Mr Titchmarsh, Dan Pearson and Monty Don. I usually read all the advice, but never follow any of it! I've watered the sandy soil in the raised beds until the water turns into puddles. Then I've added 3"-4" of the fibrous compost from the compost centre as a thick, water-retaining mulch. When I scrape back the mulch, a

week later, the soil is still damp underneath! Huzzah! The broadbeans really benefit from this approach. I've only had to spray them once for blackfly – an organic spray, of course. By the end of May, the ones sown in the autumn are ready for picking. I usually don't get any until June, which shows how warm it's been. I've used 2 x 70l bags of compost on one bed of "International Kidney" spuds. One after planting, and one for earthing up. With luck we'll actually get some potatoes this year, with all this attention they'll be good!

MAY 2nd

The asparagus is growing like crazy. So far there are no signs of the dreaded asparagus beetle. I wonder if there will be many about this year. Last year we hardly had any, so hopefully they won't have over~wintered anywhere. With their shiny red bodies they remind me of lily beetles. Asparagus is related to lilies, so I suppose the two types of beetle could be related. I will look it up ~ if I remember.

In a couple of year's time I will have to start thinking about replacing the asparagus bed. It's now 11 years' old, and if it takes 3 years before a bed really gets into full production, then I really need to plan carefully to avoid a gap. I may try a couple of different varieties, perhaps to harvest at different times.

June

halfway through the year and time to take stock.

Broad beans lots and lots of them! The "aquadulce" sown on top plot in the Autumn have been particularly good, as have "The Sutton" which were sown in the minigreenhouse at home. The blackfly only needed spraying once, so very pleased with this crop so far this season← smug!

Lettuces more reasons for smugness! Sowing them under the big cloche in February meant we had lettuces in May ~ and with very little slug damage, too. Best performers were Little Gems and Iceberg. The little Gems and 'Cos' types were also slow to bolt, despite the warm dry weather. The mixed varieties of "salad bowl" types did not perform nearly as well ~ no idea why.

Pak choi WOW! I'm a genius. The variety was from "Suffolk Herbs" and never bolted! We had over 40 plants and ate them stir-fried with garlic, or microwaved with plum sauce. Cathy said how many people had commented (I'd given her a tray of 36 plants) on hers, as they were in full view of the main path. An outstanding success!

Peas not as successful as the broad beans. The early sowings under the cloches (at the same time as the lettuces in February) started well; they raced away and looked sturdy. However, they started to fade in colour when about 8" high and sulked, never yielding more than half a dozen pods per plant.

Runner Beans have been the most challenging – EVER! Slugs ate the seedlings grown in the root-trainers in the backyard. Another sowing and set of transplants went the same way. A third attempt finally got going up the beanpoles at the end of June – but took almost a whole can of organic slug pellets to get going.

Courgettes – why am I unable to grow them??? Eve on the next plot gets so many of three plants, and also grows pumpkins the size of elephant's heads. Mine sulk, and remain shrivelled little plants, taunting me with a few flowers before getting powdery mildew and turning to a crisp of dead foliage! I simply don't get it! What am I doing wrong? Perhaps I'll buy plants next year rather than growing from seed…

The only time of year that I can tackle the compost bins is June. This is because in Winter the frogs and newts find the compost makes a snug and safe Winter home. I'd hate to injure one with the fork.

I've watered all four compost bins regularly this summer. As well as helping the compost, it stops the wasps from building nests with any dry twigs or grass in there.

Snipping all twigs and woody stems is a real pain, but it makes a big difference to how fast the garden waste turns to compost!

ALL THINGS COMPOST

COMPOST

JUNE'S BEST JOB.

This time I've been more organised than usual. I've laid black plastic down in front of the bins. I can turn the top, uncomposted layer onto this first. Hurrah!

TIME. I've come to realise that little rots down in the winter. I'm better off leaving the bins alone until this time of year. Rather than using the compost in the Spring, I know that in June it will be like crumbly chocolate, won't need sieving and can be used as a thick mulch.

I've read that you can speed up composting in the Winter by putting a plastic bottle, filled with hot water, into the middle of your compost bin. Good idea.

Illustrated as tea plates because compost is food!

Jersey Royals by the bucketful.

It reminds me of when we first got the allotment 11 years ago. Un-worked for years, the ground was incredibly fertile. Our first potatoes back then grew without any need for fertilisers. At the end of that first season we bought proper hessian sacks to store the potatoes in ~ and we filled all four sacks! The potatoes over-wintered beauti~ fully in the unheated front bedroom, lasting all the way through to the following March. We were so pleased at our success.

Runner beans ~ delicious.

The first runner beans of the year always remind me of home in Lichfield. Mum used to grow them and it was always my job to string them. I'd sit in front of "Grange Hill" with a tray, the colander, a pile of beans and a small knife. My ambition was to de-string a bean in a single, unbroken thread. This meant starting with the knife at one end of the bean, cutting along the long edge of the bean and then turning at the other end to cut down the remaining long edge. The "string" always broke at the turn! To this day I've never managed it.

Time to tackle the scarecrow.

I made her quite a few years ago. Her frame is chicken wire, which allowed me to make her very lifelike as I can manipulate her into a natural stance. I know she's lifelike because I've caught my neighbour John talking to her, thinking she's me!

JULY FIRST WEEK

She was in need of a make over as the foxes had stolen her shoes (they have a reputation for stealing your trainers if you leave them outside to air in the summer, so it must be them). It only took an hour to straighten her up and give her a change of clothes.

The schoolkids are having a tour of the allotments with their teachers. They stop at the gate to my plot and the teachers point out my scarecrow. "Look how lifelike that scarecrow is!" "No," interjects the other teacher, "we should say 'scareperson'." Heaven help those children's education...

There's a lot to juggle in order to get ready with winter crops.

At this time of year, I'm jumping through hoops trying to keep the plot watered. We have running water, but it is still a real effort to give everything enough of a drink. That having been said, applying compost as a 2" inch mulch, after watering underneath first, really has made a difference.

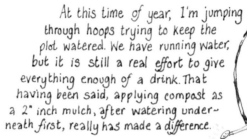

JULY

2ND WEEK

Good display of lettuces.

Trained the runner beans.

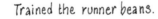

"THANK YOU" "Thank you!" "Thank you."

Jersey Royals performing well.

The squashes have all died. They are covered in white powdery mildew.

The apples have been a real success this year. I don't know what varieties they are, but one has the most incredible white flesh, & tastes very sweet.

The bindweed from the [late] Frenchman's plot is now rampant. I'm going to have to spray it.

Brock told me the Frenchman passed away a few weeks ago.

Everyone comments. We all agree that however odd & eccentric he was, he certainly knew how to get things to grow. His onions were the size of babies' heads!

The dahlias are looking particularly good this year.

The runner beans are finally under way, despite their slow start. By mid August they are at the top of the bean poles.

Emma & Sue helped me to pick at least 2 dozen runner beans mid August.

The allotment cat has made short work of the mice nesting in the compost bin. He consumed 4 at least.

YIKES!

The Swiss chard is very slow to grow. It must be all the dry conditions earlier this summer.

AUGUST

A MONTH OF VARIABLE SUNSHINE
AND LOTS OF RAIN
THE VICTORIA PLUMS HAVE BEEN
THE BEST EVER. WHEN SUE AND EMMA CAME
FOR THEIR ANNUAL VISIT, THEY HELPED TO PICK
THEM WHICH WAS A GREAT HELP, EMMA BEING SMALL ENOUGH
TO GET UNDER THE NETTING I'D PUT UP AGAINST THE BIRDS

WITH STEVE UP NORTH
FOR THE FIRST MATCH OF
THE SEASON, I SPENT TWO DAYS ALLOTMENTING
THE BINDWEED
THAT I THOUGHT WAS STARTING
TO BE UNDER CONTROL, ISN'T. I SEEM TO SPEND
MUCH OF MY TIME DEALING WITH OTHER PLOT HOLDERS WEEDS
THIS MAKES ME CRY

Not a single tomato this year.

They all got blight. They looked so healthy earlier in the season that I decided not to spray them ~ big mistake. It's such a shame as we both love home grown tomatoes ~ they are up there with asparagus and new potatoes for taste. Lesley and Philip took pity on us and gave us some of their own tomatoes. I think next year I might buy tomato plants ~ they might do better.

FREE TO GARDENERS

SEPTEMBER
Delights

30 DAYS of growing

tomatoes

at their best

CONSIDER SOWING
CUT AND COME AGAIN
SALADS FOR WINTER

"TIDY THE SHED"

Carry on
picking
dahlias

oops!

DEFROST FREER TO
MAKE ROOM FOR FRUIT

The basil has done well. I grew big pots of it at home to go with the tomatoes ~ the irony!

We've had oodles of plums ~ so many that I put several pounds of them in a basket with a "help-yourself" sign. We've had them in crumbles and stewed with rhubarb. Steve now likes rhubarb ~ and so he should given that he's a Yorkshireman from close to the famous "Rhubarb Triangle" at Wakefield. I've frozen the ~~remaining~~ remaining plums for winter.

Menu.

Scallops wrapped in bacon, cooked on the barbecue. Indian flatbreads. Lamb kebabs & cucumber dip. Salad, breads and cheeses for dessert.

Drinks.

Champagne (courtesy from Lesley and Philip).
Rosé and red wine.
Water (sparkling and still).

Theme.

Wear a hat! Last time the theme was "Merchant Ivory." It was easy for George and Donny and Lesley as they just had to find a nice floaty summer dress. Not so easy for philip and Steve ~ hence this year's theme.

Accidents.

The homemade Indian flatbreads stuck together in the heat. Oops. I roll them back into balls and Lesley leapt into action with a wine bottle to re-roll them.

Weather

Absolutely boiling. By 2pm we are fighting for the shade! We reckon it must be the hottest October day ever.

Steve tells **FLOSS** **LESLEY** **PHILIP** "say cheese."

OCTOBER
ALLOTMENT PARTY

High lights

The apples and blackberries are delicious. Plucked from the allotment moments earlier, I cut the apples in two and filled the core with blackberries then baked them.

Transportation

We took all the food to the allotment in the insulated trolley. Because it has patterned veg on it, we call it "the fruit & veg sledge!"

PESTS PREDATORS & PARROTS.

The allotment wildlife has been pretty active this month. The BADGERS dig up the lawn, looking for chafer grubs. The grubs look a bit like fat juicy prawns, So it's easy to see why the badgers tuck in.

PARAKEETS

The rumour is they escaped from the filmset (or "film set"!) of African Queen. Noisy and numerous, they monopolise the seed heads of the sunflowers now and in the Autumn.

A PEST? ME?

There are fewer RABBITS this year.

That's because we've got more foxes, in at least two dens.

Predator or PEST? Slugs are so rife on the allotment that I'm starting to think they should be re-classified as predators. Ask a lettuce, and I'm sure it would agree.

SLUGS

We also get a lot of snails. Their favourite hiding places include the corners of the cold frame and inside stacks of pots or seedtrays. Snails are easily killed by stamping on them. A short, sharp death.

I wonder if the answer is here.

I HAVE SO MANY BULBS IN POTS at home that I'm thinking about taking them up to the allotment. Planted under the dahlias, they would make a lovely show of colour in the spring. The foliage from the dahlias would then hide the old foliage from the bulbs as they die down. I've got daffodils in all shapes and sizes, grape hyacinths and tulips so it would make a good mix of colour there.

IT'S NOVEMBER, SO ONCE AGAIN there's talk on the allotments of having some sort of bonfire party. Bill and Ellie usually start the conversation, but they are giving up their plot this winter. Kathy & I discuss the pros & cons of a bonfire party and both confess we are afraid of the badgers! That's why we always go home before dusk.

KATHY IS SERIOUSLY THINKING about keeping chickens. Colin, her husband, is brilliant at woodwork so he has offered to build the hen-house for her. Their plot is next to the foxes' den, so she's naturally concerned about stress & safety. I must check if she's Kathy or Cathy.

BROAD BEAN - AQUA DULCE. BOTTOM PLOT, BED No 10. I sowed a packet of broad bean seeds directly into the bed, having forked-in some grow-more first. The mice, who over-winter in the compost bins, are a real menace when it comes to broad beans. Sometimes they eat the seeds as soon as I've sown them. More often, they wait until late winter when the plants are 4" high, then eat the seeds, chomping through the stem. I've put down holly!

ONCE AGAIN, EVE and her family on the plot next door have grown a fantastic display of pumpkins. I don't know how she does it, but every year she gets pumpkins to grow to the size of a baby elephant's head! She's also good at growing summer squashes and her courgettes are always prolific. She usually offers me as many courgettes as we can eat, so I might ask her advice. She must have a secret.

Ooh! Aah.

BROAD BEAN

November Gallery

December

Temperature. Brrr! The extra broad beans were sown as spares at home in case of frost. They were sown in homemade newspaper tubes and put in a gravel tray in the backyard. No drainage holes. They got water logged. I moved them to better drainage & they recovered- amazingly.

The ALLOTMENT HAS BEEN LEFT ALONE ALL MONTH! I have no idea what state it's in. It's been too cold and wet at the weekends to go.

GARDENING CHRISTMAS PRESENTS~
- from Mum~ a pink tub trug and two pairs of precision weeding gloves.
- from Jennie~ Felco secateurs (one can never have too many pairs) and flower snips
- from David and Hazel~ Filey Allotments Association calendar (brilliant).

Plans for next year. I'm going to buy wood to make proper raised beds. After over a decade (!) the bits of wood from skips that I used to make the original beds are pretty rotten. Some are so bad that there are toadstools growing out of them.

Tomatoes to be defended against blight.

New brassica varieties to explore.

Carrots to be sown early to avoid carrot fly invasion.

New pea varieties to be explored.

STAR SHIP ASPARAGUS

2012

AND WE HAVE LIFT-OFF. ALL SYSTEMS GO!
FOR THE
Start of the gardening year.

January

The weather is terrible! I'm itching to get to the allotment, but there really is little point when it's as cold and as miserable as this. Steve suggests driving to the livery stables at Hampton to get some manure. It's free and usually there's loads of it. We stop off first at Homebase to get some strong rubble sacks for the manure. It's fresh strawy manure which means it's got to be stacked for at least 6 months before it can be used on the allotment.

Filling the 8 sacks takes a while, but once it's done, we drive up to the allotment. The car is a bit smelly by this point! With Steve's help, I wheelbarrow the sacks of manure up the long steep path to our plot. The weather doesn't seem so bad now, so I ask Steve if he minds if I spend an hour pottering on the allotment.

DOO BE DOO

SPLISH

WHAT ARE YOU DOING?!

SPLOSH

HOME

I don't have my watch or my mobile phone so it's not long before I've lost all track of time. The weather has now changed. Cold rain is pouring down, almost like sleet.

I'm determined to get one of the compost bins emptied so that I can stack at least some of the manure. It takes ages to empty one bin, spread the compost into the other bins and then start to fork the manure into the empty bin.

I nearly jump out of my skin when Steve appears, carrying the big golfing umbrella. He points out that I've been gone for over THREE hours! My waterproof isn't waterproof. I'm chilled to the bone. And I still have to find somewhere to stack the remaining 3 bags of manure. Oh well, at least we have enough manure for our spuds.

LABOURS
of the months.

a medieval theme for the
cold weather, in anticipation
of the hard work of spring

"Oops. Spelling Fairy
required to spell "hard."
Hardly a difficult word!"

FLOSS HAS INVENTED A SPELLING FAIRY
TO POINT OUT ANY MISTAKES, BUT THE FAIRY
HAS AN ATTITUDE THAT FLOSS DOESN'T LIKE.

Second week of February and it's a cold day on Saturday.

We took two bags of compost up to the allotment but they split when we unloaded them. The only way to get them out of the boot was to shovel them, a spadeful at a time into the wheelbarrow. The reason they'd split was they were wet. This also made them very heavy! I nearly ran myself over with the barrow as it rolled back down the slope at the cemetery gate.

The compost was spread on the bed by the greengage tree and the dahlia bed by the shed. I read somewhere that they-dahlias-are heavy feeders so this year I am going to give them a bit more care. I've bought a yellow and orange type which I am starting off in trays in the greenhouse.

Washed the greenhouse, as well as the coldframe, with diluted bleach.

I'm not sure the medieval look works for me.

A day of hard labour.

Added compost to the asparagus bed, and to two of the beds on the bottom plot.
Weeded the remaining beds on the bottom plot.
Snipped away the bindweed from fruit cage

"Hmm. The recipe suggests more cheese. I wonder where the Two-Legs keep it …"

Potatoes

My seed potatoes are eaten by a mouse who is living in the spare bedroom. Great. Destroyed before I've even planted them!

FEBRUARY
5th.

Weeded all the paths on the bottom half of the allotment. The nigella self-seeds like crazy and always seems to survive the winter.

Removed...

... All of the remaining strawberries except 5 which are now potted up in the greenhouse. Hopefully they are out of reach of the badgers and birds.

... All the remaining asparagus fern. Used them to insulate the dahlias from frosts

... The last of the dahlia stems and dug up the big yellow verbascum. It was over 8 feet tall with a root that looked like a big devil's claw! Very sinister-looking.

Weather.

Sunny. A balmy 5°c but it felt much warmer than that in the sunshine.

A tale of optimism

Hmm... I wonder if it's warm enough for the allotment today?

AND NOW, THE WEATHER

WHAT IS SHE DOING??? She's drawn us as SIAMESE!

IT'S SATURDAY MORNING.

WAIT FOR US! WE'RE NEARLY READY.

Swift tying of scarf.

GARGLE!

FLOSS GETS WRAPPED UP, BUT FIRST...

... SHE HAS TO BRING IN THE COMPOST WHICH HAS GOT WET AND IS HEAVY.

ARGH!

WET and HEAVY COMPOST

LET ME SEE WHAT I CAN SOW IN FEBRUARY. AH, CAULIFLOWERS, SWEET PEAS, MUSHY PEAS, SWISS CHARD, COURGETTES.

IS THAT MOUSE UNDER THERE?

I'LL SORT MY TREATS

SEEDS

TREATS

EXHAUSTED BY DRAGGING THE COMPOST BACK INSIDE, FLOSS DECIDES TO STAY AT HOME. THERE'S MUCH TO BE DONE.

1st PRIZE

GLEAMING TROPHY

Ooh, I love a good dig.

BEANS! Please sow BEANS

THE GIRLS LIKE TO BE INVOLVED AS FLOSS STARTS PRICKING OUT, POTTING ON AND SOWING FOR THE SPRING.

I'm sure this will be the BEST year yet on the allotment.

FRUIT

Cheese always gives me funny dreams.

WORN OUT WITH PLANNING, PLANTING, POTTING AND POTTERING, FLOSS RETIRES WITH RUBY FOR A NAP. 2012 WILL BE A GOOD YEAR FOR VEGETABLES.